A ROMANCE

A Romance

by

Bruce Weigl

University of Pittsburgh Press

Published by the University of Pittsburgh Press, Pittsburgh, Pa. 15260
Copyright © 1979, Bruce Weigl
All rights reserved
Feffer and Simons, Inc., London
Manufactured in the United States of America

Library of Congress Cataloging in Publication Data

Weigl, Bruce, 1949–
 A romance.

 (Pitt poetry series)
 I. Title.
 PZ4.W4195Ro   [PS3573.E3835]   811'.5'4   78-23603
 ISBN 0-8229-3393-4
 ISBN 0-8229-5303-X pbk.

Acknowledgment is made to the following publications for permission to re-
print poems that appear in this book: *The Back Door, Big Moon, Field, The
New Honolulu Review, Quarterly West, The Sam Houston Literary Review,*
and *Some.*

"Strawberries" first appeared in *Poetry Now.*

The poems "Sailing to Bien Hoa" and "The String Quartet" appeared origi-
nally in *The Western Humanities Review.*

"Hand to Hand," "Monkey," "Short," and "Anna Grasa" first appeared in
Ironwood. Along with "On This Spot," "4th of July, Toledo, Ohio," and "Exe-
cutioner on Holiday," they form part of the chapbook *Executioner,* published
in 1976 by Ironwood Press, P.O. Box 40907, Tucson, AZ 85717.

"Blue Coda," "Feather Pictures," "Points of Coincidence," "Song of Identi-
ties," and "Sparrows" originally appeared in the chapbook *A Sackfull of Old
Quarrels,* published in 1977 by The Cleveland State University Poetry Center.
Used by permission of Alberta T. Turner, Editor.

The publication of this book is supported by a grant from the National Endowment for the Arts in Washington, D.C., a Federal agency.

for Jean
and for Anna Grasa

CONTENTS

Sailing to Bien Hoa   3
Fourth of July: Toledo, Ohio   4
Hand to Hand   5
A Romance   6
Pigeons   8
The Sharing   9
Feather Pictures   10
On This Spot   12
Sparrows   13
The First Word   14
Monkey   15
Short   20
The String Quartet   21
The Garden   22
Convoy   23
Milk Prose   24
When Saigon Was French   25
Mica Farm   26
Immigrants   27
Cardinal   28
The Man Who Made Me Love Him   29
Him, on the Bicycle   30
Faye   31
Points of Coincidence   32
Mines   33
Eclipse   34
The Life Before Fear   35
Blue Coda   36

Strawberries   37

Executioner on Holiday   38

Song of Identities   40

Dogs   41

I Have Had My Time Rising and Singing   43

Anna Grasa   45

Painting on a T'ang Dynasty Water Vessel   46

The Harp   47

A ROMANCE

It still has not been born,
it is both music and the word,
and therefore of all living things
the indestructible connection.

Osip Mandelstam

And it was like swimming for a
moment—that moment of cool
green coasting when you've
jumped.

William H. Gass
from *Omensetter's Luck*

SAILING TO BIEN HOA

In my dream of the hydroplane
I'm sailing to Bien Hoa
the shrapnel in my thighs
like tiny glaciers.
I remember a flower,
a kite, a mannikin playing the guitar,
a yellow fish eating a bird, a truck
floating in urine, a rat carrying a banjo,
a fool counting the cards, a monkey praying,
a procession of whales, and far off
two children eating rice,
speaking French —
I'm sure of the children,
their damp flutes,
the long line of their vowels.

FOURTH OF JULY: TOLEDO, OHIO

So many flags today
hanging dead on thin poles
stuck in the front lawns of my neighbors.

The folks next door have a flag,
a boat, station wagon,
and a twelve-year-old kid screaming,
holding up one burnt mangled thumb.
He hung on a moment too long
to the tiny explosive.
He screams loud

but his father,
a man I know and dislike,
looks up from the barbecue
and spits out his cigar in disgust.
His wife ignores them both
because she is frail,
because she is trying
to keep the paper plates
from lifting off the table.

My people are no different:
the old man is inside
listening to Wally and the Walleyes
jam to the "Beer Barrel Polka."

But it's no good.
I didn't listen,
I don't remember what he said
when he turned up the radio,
spun me around half full of love
half full of the need
to pin me down.

HAND TO HAND

We sit in a circle around First Sergeant. Who wants to try me he says and my hand goes up and before I know what I'm doing I'm doing it. He slams me into the ground like someone made of water — my back, my lungs, some clouds. I take his hand and he spins me and I'm down again. I can feel the day lost, the night I'm in my rack hurt, unable to sleep, he comes gentle like so much man, leads me past the fire guard, past fifty sleeping soldiers, pushes his bunk aside, pulls me and we dance and I learn hand to hand brothers, learn the places on the body that betray. . . . Close my eyes. Open them. Fall violently upward.

A ROMANCE

The skinny red-haired girl gets up
from the bar and dances
over to the juke box
and punches the buttons as if
she were playing the piano —
below the white points of her pelvis
an enormous belt buckle
shaped like the head of a snake
with two red rhinestone eyes
which she polishes with the heels of her hands
making circles on her own fine thighs
and looking up
she catches me staring, my lust like a flag
waving at her across the room
as her big mean boy friend
runs hillbilly after hillbilly off the table
in paycheck nine-ball games.

It is always like this with me in bars,
wanting women I know
I'll have to get my face
punched bloody to love.
Or she could be alone,
and I could be dull enough from liquor
to imagine my face interesting enough to take her
into conversation while I count my money
hoping to jesus I have enough
to get us both romantic.
I don't sleep anyway so I go to bars
and tell my giant lies to women
who have heard them from me,

from the thousands of me
out on the town with our impossible strategies
for no good reason but our selves,
who are holy.

PIGEONS

There's a man standing
in a coop,
his face is wet.
He says he's too old:
"You can't give them away
they just come back."
I follow him to the cellar.
Latin blessings on the wall,
sauerkraut in barrels,
he puts his arm around my waist
begins to make a noise,
pigeons bleeding.
We're both crying now
he moves his tongue around,
pulls feathers from his coat.
A fantail he says,
the kind that hop around
and don't fly well.

THE SHARING

I have not ridden a horse much,
two, maybe three times,
a broken gray mare my cousin called Ghost.
Then only in the fall
through the flat pastures of Ohio.
That's not much,
but I watched two Chinese tanks
roll out of the jungle side by side,
their turret guns feeling before them
like a man walking through his dream,
their tracks slapping the bamboo like hooves.

I can't name the gaits of a horse
except the canter,
and that rocks you high to the withers,
but I saw those arms,
those guns and did not know for a moment
what they were, but knew they were not horses
as they pulled themselves deep
into the triple-canopy jungle
until there was only the dull rattle of their tracks
and a boy on a gray horse,
flying through the opening fields.

FEATHER PICTURES

My mother bought two pictures
from a blind man
who carried himself
door to door in my town.

Made with green, red, and brown
feathers he stuck together:
ugly pictures of birds

flying through his eyes.
All his nights
lying in bed
the radio between stations,
the room above him alive,
women he imagines dancing,
coming down to him. . . .
His bed shaking with his rocking,

rocking the cradles
of his eyes,
he thinks he is close
to seeing.
The lids ache
and there's a picture:
birds preening,
perched on the ladder's
missing rung
pulling feathers
through their mouths.

The woman next door said
if you didn't buy,
if you slammed the door
in his face
he'd be there in the morning
pulling feathers from a fat robin,
tapping nails into a frame
torn from your door.

ON THIS SPOT

This is where the old woman lifted her dress, pulled down her stiff underwear and pissed in the alley. I was standing in the dark cooling my heels. She didn't see me as she came through the door, squatted next to the bar owner's white El Dorado. I'm glad she didn't see me. I'm glad I watched her piss so hard her eyes closed. When she finished and wiped herself with the handkerchief and pulled the dress down around her thick ankles, I almost called to her.

SPARROWS

Yes it was raining the day we wrecked the convertible.
I pretended to sleep while you led us home
across a large body of water.
You must have carried me
or pulled me on my back by my chin —
I can float but can't swim.
I woke at your father's house.
We can sleep you said,
we can make love,
but there was the sound of birds
scratching at the window
and you helped me up to watch them huddling,
their brown chests catching the light.
Then, yes the ambulance
yes my shock
yes the blood
going hard and cold
with my love of believing we come back
from those waters and that silence
to sing and to touch the new life.

THE FIRST WORD

for Andrew

Burn is the first word.
Two dawns burning
in the mouth of the great plains,
silos levitated by the heat,

and the sky burns
above the even lyric of crickets
in the dawn,
the first word

and the last word,
burn,
and the drinkers of stars
come out.

MONKEY

"Out of the horror there rises a musical ache that is beautiful . . ."

James Wright

1

I am you are he she it is
they are you are we are.
I am you are he she it is
they are you are we are.
When they ask for your number
pretend to be breathing.
Forget the stinking jungle,
force your fingers between the lines.
Learn to get out of the dew.
The snakes are thirsty.
Bladders, water, boil it, drink it.
Get out of your clothes:
you can't move in your green clothes.
Your O.D. in color issue.
Get out the plates and those who ate,
those who spent the night.
Those small Vietnamese soldiers.
They love to hold your hand.
Back away from their dark cheeks.
Small Vietnamese soldiers.
They love to love you.
I have no idea how it happened,
I remember nothing but light.

2

I don't remember the hard
swallow of the lover.
I don't remember the burial of ears.
I don't remember
the time of the explosion.
This is the place curses are manufactured:
delivered like white tablets.
The survivor is spilling his bedpan.
He slips a curse into your pocket,
you're finally satisfied.
I don't remember the heat
in the hands,
the heat around the neck.

Good times bad times sleep
get up work. Sleep get up
good times bad times.
Work eat sleep good bad work times.
I like a certain cartoon of wounds.
The water which refused to dry.
I like a little unaccustomed mercy.
Pulling the trigger is all we have.
I hear a child.

3

I dropped to the bottom of a well.
I have a knife.
I cut someone with it.
Oh, I have the petrified eyebrows
of my Vietnam monkey.
My monkey from Vietnam.
My monkey.
Put your hand here.
It makes no sense.
I beat the monkey.
I didn't know him.
He was bloody.
He lowered his intestines
to my shoes. My shoes
spit-shined the moment
I learned to tie the bow.
I'm not on speaking terms
with anyone. In the wrong climate
a person can spoil,
the way a pair of boots slows you down. . . .

I don't know when I'm sleeping.
I don't know if what I'm saying
is anything at all.
I'll lie on my monkey bones.

4

I'm tired of the rice
falling in slow motion
like eggs from the smallest animal.
I'm twenty-five years old,
quiet, tired of the same mistakes,
the same greed, the same past.
The same past with its bleat
and pound of the dead,
with its hand grenade
tossed into a hootch on a dull Sunday
because when a man dies like that
his eyes sparkle,
his nose fills with witless nuance
because a farmer in Bong Son
has dead cows lolling
in a field of claymores
because the VC tie hooks to their comrades
because a spot of blood
is a number
because a woman is lifting
her dress across the big pond.

If we're soldiers we should smoke them
if we have them. Someone's bound
to point us in the right direction
sooner or later.

I'm tired and I'm glad you asked.

5

There is a hill.
Men run top hill.
Men take hill.
Give hill to man.

*

Me and my monkey
and me and my monkey
my Vietnamese monkey
my little brown monkey
came with me
to Guam and Hawaii
in Ohio he saw
my people he
jumped on my daddy
he slipped into mother
he baptized my sister
he's my little brown monkey
he came here from heaven
to give me his spirit imagine
my monkey my beautiful
monkey he saved me lifted
me above the punji
sticks above the mines
above the ground burning
above the dead above
the living above the
wounded dying the wounded
dying.

* *

Men take hill away from smaller men.
Men take hill and give to fatter man.
Men take hill. Hill has number.
Men run up hill. Run down.

19

SHORT

There's a bar girl on Trung Hung Do who has half a ten piaster note I tore in my drunken relief to be leaving the country. She has half and I have half, if I can find it. If I lost it, it wasn't on purpose, it's all I have to remember her. She has a wet sheet, a PX fan, PX radio, and half a ten piaster note, as if she cared to remember me. She thought it was stupid to tear money and when I handed it to her she turned to another soldier, new in country, who needed a girl. I hope I burn in hell.

THE STRING QUARTET

I didn't hear classical music growing up except the Mario Lanza record my father played nights he couldn't sleep. I have trouble with centuries, something about the first violin turning the great composer around to face the mute applause, Beethoven.

I was not taught music as a child. My father sang in the morning and once the old woman upstairs stood in our door and wept for what she said was the prettiest song she ever heard.

I picked up a violin once and wanted to smash it so I put it back down. I still sit at the piano and long to play the blues. They wouldn't even force me, but there is something in the language of a family, a song from another place, another country of gray workers destined to become immigrants, our ancestors who gathered with torches at the river to wish their unborn children well and to sing, long into the night.

THE GARDEN

for Dave Smith

I let the garden go dark with weeds
so thick and blossoming
they become the garden, and tonight
as I kneel in the dirt again
what I must have felt when I planted is gone.
But once I stood in a plowed field
when I was a boy
and heard the river call me and ran to it
balancing on the clay-slick of mounds
the plow turned over.
I ran until I fell then rolled in the dirt
until it took me.
I did not know I wanted to bless my life,
not then, but tonight I pull
at the tops of heaven trees, hoe the ground black
and spread the sweet manure.
I think I made it to the river that night
because it was spring.
I waded waist deep
to meet my shadow where the moon
through the oaks fell on dark water,
because a boy caught running himself wildly
through someone else's plowed field
must know something,
a boy who gives himself to the river
in the spring of his boyhood
must see the woman in him,
he must see the mole
spin its shadow in quiet tunneling,
his sole purpose
to go as far from the light as possible.

CONVOY

On a convoy from Bong Son to Hue we stop at a Vietnamese graveyard. People set up shelter halves right over the top of gravestones: one rock wall just in case. It's raining, I smell people.

Two in the morning someone wakes me for guard. I'm out of bed, standing in the cold. The man next to me walks over to talk. A helicopter is parked thirty yards in front of us and in the moon it begins to move. My friend becomes leader, he wants to fire, I'm afraid of an explosion. He tells me to circle the ship while he covers.

At the window it's dark, no moon. Inside, the pilot, restlessly turning in his sleep, rocking his ship.

MILK PROSE

My mother brings me milk. A silver bucket hangs from her hands. She says it's easier to carry two. Occasionally she stumbles, the weeds are thick and though the field looks level, it isn't. A little milk spills, runs down the sides of the buckets, coats her hands.

When the milk spills she twitches. She doesn't stop. She sets the milk in front of me, rolls the sleeves of her dress, brushes back her hair, goes to her knees and dips milk with cups she makes with her hands. She is beautiful when she does this. After three or four drinks she lifts the dress, wipes my mouth.

WHEN SAIGON WAS FRENCH

I remember Francoise crossing
the room in a naked blur
in the hotel on Trung Hung Do —
dark except for flares
falling in the cemetery
catching on the window
as if the caches of weapons would be visible.
She was looking for something, a cigarette
or some more clothes, it was her idiosyncrasy
to move around afterwards
as it was mine to lie still
with the understanding that this was a war
in which no one was called to duty,
a war with no fronts.
I was a day away from leaving
and didn't want to go — a boy
come six thousand miles from Ohio
to fall in with a French girl,
to lord over my block of the black market
and spend my money on cocaine,
all that beautiful dying
when Saigon was French.

MICA FARM

1

Except when he's standing empty-handed in front of his house trailer, or kneeling in the sawdust milking his slack-in-the-ass goat, I don't see Lester, my neighbor, I see his sons. The oldest is slim and tight, chases a foundered pony, hooves grown up and split into hard curls. The youngest son's smile is impossible to avoid. At night it lights the woods. I imagine him leading men much older through the trees to my window. When I look out I see hundreds of smiling, fiery faces. My wife says he's a happy boy.

2

The barn is cool except for the breath of horses. In the morning and at night I feed two horses. Horses don't stare or vomit. I remember in 1963 Edith Buell was thrown from her horse and broke her neck. After the hospital she wanted to ride. She couldn't walk, they carried her, eased her onto the warm withers. There's a place on the front of a horse, behind the neck, where the shoulder begins, fits the catheter perfectly.

3

For a long time I stood in front of the barn. I suspected the old woman to be staring from her bedroom full of memories wishing things on me: bad children and whiskey. Salt on the porch and you're dead. Her fists clenched inside out across her breasts shaking all the words loose from her mouth. In the barn she hands me the hammer, hand-forged and rusty; and the nail she straightened on the concrete; and the picture of a girl in wheat. She stretches on her toes, points to a spot, wait. My left is your right, why? Because you're hammering.

IMMIGRANTS

I have gone home to the alleys
with their rabbit hutches
with their fat white rabbits
beside tin shacks
where old men pee
on the quiet end of evening.
But home, I am still lost,
out too late
where the street bleeds,
where the bright bus slides by
and the smoke from many slag heaps
hangs low above the glow of blast furnaces.

It is 3 A.M. and the migrations
back and forth on this street of bars
have thinned to the few of us left
watching it grow dark
bar light after bar light.
Down the long mill street
those who punch the clock early
must be stirring in their sleep.
I am glad I am not yet one of them.
I will be in bed by first light, asleep
by first blood.

CARDINAL

She is more beautiful than all her red husbands,
more indifferent toward the dry seeds on the window.
You don't notice by her color though the gray is perfect gray,
nor by her song though it cuts through you,
not even by the way she flits upward branch to branch,
female shape ascending inside the shuddering tree —
it's her head, the way she tilts it side to side,
pure movement, lifting when the wind catches
her small belly as she leans but doesn't let go.

THE MAN WHO MADE ME LOVE HIM

All I know about this man
is that he played the trumpet
from his bedroom window.
Evenings we could hear him
trying to play something
while we laughed at the din
and called him names.

I want to sing about this
but all I know
is that it was near dark
so I missed the way home
and stopped to rest in the churchyard
where gold carp lolled in the holy pond.

I was seven and the man who played the trumpet
took me to the roundhouse
where he said the hobos slept,
and though I knew the tracks
and the woods surrounding them,
I didn't know that secret.

He made me take him into my mouth,
my face rose and fell with his hips
and the sun cut through boxcars
waiting to be emptied.

HIM, ON THE BICYCLE

"There was no light; there was no light at all . . ."
Roethke

In a liftship near Hue
the door gunner is in a trance.
He's that driver who falls
asleep at the wheel
between Pittsburgh and Cleveland
staring at the Ho Chi Minh trail.

Flares fall,
where the river leaps
I go stiff,
I have to think, tropical.

The door gunner sees movement,
the pilot makes small circles:
four men running, carrying rifles,
one man on a bicycle.

He pulls me out of the ship,
there's firing far away.
I'm on the back of the bike
holding his hips.
It's hard pumping for two,
I hop off and push the bike.

I'm brushing past trees,
the man on the bike stops pumping,
lifts his feet,
we don't waste a stroke.
His hat flies off,
I catch it behind my back,
put it on, I want to live forever!

Like a blaze
streaming down the trail.

FAYE

Down the ruined stairs through the back lot
past the church with its high rock altar,
through the slag heaps rolling like dunes by the tracks
where I would sometimes find a flare burning
and carry it down the gravel road
to the river I swam as a boy.

I never saw Faye at the river
when Gus and fat Tom and I
swam naked in the moon,
but if she went in where they say,
where they found her claw marks in the steep bank
the current must have taken her
to the rooted bottom
and held her there, pale, her blond hair swept back.

I am afraid of water since then,
and though I abandoned myself there
three times afterwards,
I did it close to the bank
and shook with the cold recollection
of the diver, his thumb held high,
the good sign that he'd found her.

POINTS OF COINCIDENCE

My grandmother is on her knees
washing the sidewalk
in front of her brown shingled house,
two three four five Livingston.

Two pine trees, their knots
like closed eyes.
Oh, she has a white dress,
dark pockets.

The old man is in the back yard
shaking his cane at the rabbits.
He's penning them for the night
but he's in no hurry.

The dishes are done.
She took off her apron.
He put down the cane.
All day I have waited,

I want to sit with them and drink.
Already the evening gathers
with just a slip of moon.
Heart, don't fail me now.

MINES

1

In Vietnam I was always afraid of mines:
North Vietnamese mines, Vietcong mines,
French mines, American mines,
whole fields marked with warning signs.

A Bouncing Betty comes up waist high —
cuts you in half.
One man's legs were laid
alongside him in the Dustoff,
he asked for a chairback, morphine,
he screamed he wanted to give
his eyes away, his kidneys,
his heart . . .

2

Here is how you walk at night: slowly lift
one leg, clear the sides with your arms, clear the back,
front, put the leg down, like swimming.

ECLIPSE

for my father

1

One dusk when the streets were empty
I was drifting in an empty lot
playing a silent war game with myself
my WW II leather pilot's hat muting blast furnaces
that groaned in my town

2

I won't tell you that my father and his father
who punched the card in and out every day
loved their lives — they worked hard and bitched
and got nothing, and gave little
except the hats of thick skin.
Yet there was a motion,
once as my mother leaned in the light-ruled doorway
watching night birds sweep and pass
upward catching the light, and once
as I stood in an empty lot,
and the sky went suddenly dark and I watched
what I knew I was not supposed to watch.

3

I did not know what was happening to me
caught in that huge shadow
struck dumb and staring into the fiery dark
until my father came from nowhere and lifted me
without breaking his long stride.

We sat on the porch that evening, watched it rain.
The green army blanket wrapped us
and mist, like skin unraveling,
rose from his white shoulders.

THE LIFE BEFORE FEAR

When Acey O'Neil smacked his brother Herbert
on the side of his head with a two-by-four
I thought Herbert would die,
but he didn't even bleed,
he just lay there, dulled out some
and shook as though whipped with joy.
And then he got up.
He let us feel the lump on his head
not so much out of goodness,
as out of a need to be touched.
After we each had a turn
Herbert raised his face
and wandered off stiffly
like a man who hears his name
called across a great distance.

BLUE CODA

I've begun to hear
the weeping of beautiful men,
it grows loud
the way my fear of women
grows deep.

Whoever you were in whatever
bar that was, it felt good
when you put your hand on my shoulder.

Now I'm alone because I couldn't
talk with you,
I didn't know what to say,
you're a man.

Across the road
a field of corn beckons me
but I can't move,

I can only close my eyes
and see you
swimming through the cornflowers,
reaching for me, now.

STRAWBERRIES

She was washing strawberries in the white sink
and I turned my back on her to measure something
about the afternoon, and how it had not chosen us
and she disappeared.

The color of strawberries in the sink,
the color of peaches cut in thin moons,
the white and dry banana, the apple, the grape.
The color of mud on her ankles,
the paleness of her ankles,
the paleness of her thighs,
the color of her hair printed on her face,
the paleness of her face,
her black hair.

She is turning in the door again,
she is back from the garden and in the course of things
she washes strawberries.

EXECUTIONER ON HOLIDAY

One melancholy ghost after another
parades by my window.
Rain falls like wax beans.
Key moves in the lock.

When I can't sleep
I drink laudanum —
the cocktail of insomnia,
then I sleep too long,

the only thing moving
on my body
is a thin layer of dust
rising each time

the doctor pounds my chest:
sleeping sickness he says,
dull fly bite.

But now there's a new disease,
I don't know if I'm
awake or asleep,

one day I'm back in the army,
a nameless private in a crack
platoon. We never see the enemy
yet we have wonderful statistics.

Next day a crippled friend
walks across the room,
tells me his paralysis was unreal,
thin steel sliver.

Occasionally in this zone
I'm handed a mirror.
I look at my face,
find it gaunt but interesting,

my eyes are innocent
without passion or desire,
my smile slightly twisted.

SONG OF IDENTITIES

My father, a good man,
can't look my wife in the face.
She's Japanese. He was in that war
on a boat dumping fire
into people's kitchens.

Guam, Wake, the lovely Midways
rising out of the fog two miles
off the bow of the USS *Nevada*
while the governor passed out
silver dollars on deck.

My wife, embarrassed,
says she's no more Japanese than I am,
but once while she lay asleep
I swear the word *Nippon*
formed on her lips.

We'll have brown babies,
dark eyes moist and clear
behind that serious flap of skin.
My father will father them in his longing,
and Hirohito, drunk on the shadows of flowers,
will rock them through his gardens.

DOGS

I bought a bar girl in Saigon
cigarettes, watches, and Tide soap
to sell on the black market
and she gave me a room to sleep in
and all the cocaine I could live through
those nights I had to leave.
I would sometimes meet them, on the stairs,
and she would be wrapped in the soldier
who was always drunk, smiling,
her smell all over him.

She ran once to the room screaming
about dogs and pulled me down to the street
where a crowd of Vietnamese gathered
watching two stuck.
The owners fought about whose fault it was.
The owner of the male took off his sandal,
began to beat the female;
the owner of the female
kicked the male
but they did not part,
the beating made her tighten
and her tightening made him swell
as she dragged him down the street
the crowd running after them.

I remembered my grandfather,
how his pit bull locked up
the same way with the neighbor's dog.
The neighbor screamed and kicked
and the cop with his nightstick

sucked his teeth and circled
the dogs as the dogs circled.
Yet my grandfather knew what to do —
not cold water, warm,
warm and pour it slow.

I HAVE HAD MY TIME
RISING AND SINGING

When I was two I crawled out
onto the ruined landing
in the red apartment building
next to the Catholic church
where I would grow up mean and steal
quarters from the holy pond.
I was a late walker
and at two I still hugged the floor
as the dizzy man hugs the ground
after spinning too long in a dance.
At the time I'm sure it was fear
but now I'm grown and say it was
more that I wanted to *know* the ground before I gave it up,
and besides, I was a fast crawler
and could tear across the room before my sister
who walked early, who ran when I was born.
I don't remember why I was on the landing,
why I crawled away from my mother.
I don't even remember the fall —
but the hanging on as I fell
my fingernails filling with splinters,
and I remember the doctor,
and the two nurses, and my father
holding me down as they pulled the splinters out,
and I imagine my screaming,
how it must have come on its own,
how it must have lasted
until we were all pale, all sobbing
until I was lifted to the back seat of my father's car
my head cradled in my mother's hands until sleep
lulled me from the pain to the memory of pain.
This, I think, is what is wrong with me.

I think this is why I *run* down stairs
as if to outrun the falling I'm certain is near,
as if to outlive the darkness I know I must have seen,
as if to survive, as I once did,
on one more span of stairs,
beautifully disguised to myself
as a child.

ANNA GRASA

I came home from Vietnam.
My father had a sign
made at the foundry:
WELCOME HOME BRUCE
in orange glow paint.
He rented spotlights,
I had to squint.
WELCOME HOME BRUCE.

Out of the car I moved
up on the sign
dreaming myself full,
the sign that cut the sky,
my eyes burned.

But behind the terrible thing
I saw my grandmother,
beautiful Anna Grasa.
I couldn't tell her, tell her.

I clapped to myself,
clapped to the sound of her dress.
I could have put it on
she held me so close,
both of us could be inside.

PAINTING ON A T'ANG DYNASTY
WATER VESSEL

Small girl leading a horse
its heavy lathered thighs steaming upward
dwarfing her at awkward angles
she is stopped
as if by some urgent recollection,
bundle of white flowers in her free hand.
Beyond her the moon before the willows
the boat of drunken fishermen and mountains,
green peaks on the neck,
on the farthest peak
two men trying to say good-bye,
one with a gift of thanks
the other gazing down the path
to his house lit by a single lamp
and his wife kneeling by the cooking
and his daughter leading a horse
its . . . no, I've come around,
this thing has turned completely around in my hands.
Someone must have meant this,
they painted it so
when you picked it up
hundreds of years later
you'd find the girl
waiting for her father
on the mountains past the loud willows
in the moon.

THE HARP

When he was my age and I was already a boy
my father made a machine in the garage.
A wired piece of steel
with many small and beautiful welds
ground so smooth they resembled rows of pearls.

He went broke with whatever it was.
He held it so carefully in his arms.
He carried it foundry to foundry.
I think it was his harp,
I think it was what he longed to make
with his hands for the world.

He moved it finally from the locked closet
to the bedroom
to the garage again
where he hung it on the wall
until I climbed and pulled it down
and rubbed it clean
and tried to make it work.

PITT POETRY SERIES
Ed Ochester, General Editor

Dannie Abse, *Collected Poems*
Adonis, *The Blood of Adonis*
Jack Anderson, *The Invention of New Jersey*
Jack Anderson, *Toward the Liberation of the Left Hand*
Jon Anderson, *Death & Friends*
Jon Anderson, *In Sepia*
Jon Anderson, *Looking for Jonathan*
John Balaban, *After Our War*
Gerald W. Barrax, *Another Kind of Rain*
Robert Coles, *A Festering Sweetness: Poems of American People*
Leo Connellan, *First Selected Poems*
Michael Culross, *The Lost Heroes*
Fazıl Hüsnü Dağlarca, *Selected Poems*
James Den Boer, *Learning the Way*
James Den Boer, *Trying to Come Apart*
Norman Dubie, *Alehouse Sonnets*
Norman Dubie, *In the Dead of the Night*
Stuart Dybek, *Brass Knuckles*
Odysseus Elytis, *The Axion Esti*
John Engels, *Blood Mountain*
John Engels, *The Homer Mitchell Place*
John Engels, *Signals from the Safety Coffin*
Abbie Huston Evans, *Collected Poems*
Brendan Galvin, *The Minutes No One Owns*
Brendan Galvin, *No Time for Good Reasons*
Gary Gildner, *Digging for Indians*
Gary Gildner, *First Practice*
Gary Gildner, *Nails*
Gary Gildner, *The Runner*
Mark Halperin, *Backroads*
Patricia Hampl, *Woman Before an Aquarium*
Michael S. Harper, *Dear John, Dear Coltrane*
Michael S. Harper, *Song: I Want a Witness*
John Hart, *The Climbers*
Samuel Hazo, *Blood Rights*
Samuel Hazo, *Once for the Last Bandit: New and Previous Poems*
Samuel Hazo, *Quartered*
Gwen Head, *Special Effects*
Gwen Head, *The Ten Thousandth Night*
Milne Holton and Graham W. Reid, eds., *Reading the Ashes: An Anthology of the Poetry of Modern Macedonia*

Milne Holton and Paul Vangelisti, eds., *The New Polish Poetry: A Bilingual Collection*

David Huddle, *Paper Boy*

Shirley Kaufman, *The Floor Keeps Turning*

Shirley Kaufman, *From One Life to Another*

Shirley Kaufman, *Gold Country*

Abba Kovner, *A Canopy in the Desert: Selected Poems*

Paul-Marie Lapointe, *The Terror of the Snows: Selected Poems*

Larry Levis, *Wrecking Crew*

Jim Lindsey, *In Lieu of Mecca*

Tom Lowenstein, tr., *Eskimo Poems from Canada and Greenland*

Archibald MacLeish, *The Great American Fourth of July Parade*

Peter Meinke, *The Night Train and The Golden Bird*

James Moore, *The New Body*

Carol Muske, *Camouflage*

Gregory Pape, *Border Crossings*

Thomas Rabbitt, *Exile*

Belle Randall, *101 Different Ways of Playing Solitaire and Other Poems*

Ed Roberson, *Etai-Eken*

Ed Roberson, *When Thy King Is A Boy*

Eugene Ruggles, *The Lifeguard in the Snow*

Dennis Scott, *Uncle Time*

Herbert Scott, *Groceries*

Richard Shelton, *The Bus to Veracruz*

Richard Shelton, *Of All the Dirty Words*

Richard Shelton, *The Tattooed Desert*

Richard Shelton, *You Can't Have Everything*

Gary Soto, *The Elements of San Joaquin*

Gary Soto, *The Tale of Sunlight*

David Steingass, *American Handbook*

David Steingass, *Body Compass*

Tomas Tranströmer, *Windows & Stones: Selected Poems*

Alberta T. Turner, *Learning to Count*

Alberta T. Turner, *Lid and Spoon*

Marc Weber, *48 Small Poems*

Bruce Weigl, *A Romance*

David P. Young, *The Names of a Hare in English*

David P. Young, *Sweating Out the Winter*